God's Guiding Light of Peace

Strength to Stand Through Life's Storms

Poetry from the Heart Collection

Volume 5

By C. Melita Webb

Copyright © 2019 by C. Melita Webb

All rights reserved. This book or any portion thereof may not be reproduced or used in any manner whatsoever without the express written permission of the author except for the use of brief quotations in a book review.

All rights reserved. Including the right to reproduce this book or portions there of, in any form. No part of this text may be reproduced, distributed, or transmitted in any form without the express written permission of the author.

Content Editors: Ruth B. Hill and Emogene Price
Copy Editor: Todd Larson

Cover design: SelfPubBookCovers.com LaLimaDesign
Chapter art: pixabay.com

Preface

Hello, and thank you for purchasing *God's Guiding Light of Peace*, Volume 5 of the Poetry from the Heart collection. In each volume we share some of the thoughts, quotes, poems, prayers, affirmations and essays that live in my heart and in my mind.
It is always an honor to spend time with you through these inspirational books.

Imagine going to sleep with joy in your heart, resting comfortably, knowing how deeply our Heavenly Father loves you, then waking up, ready to take on your day with a smile in your spirit. That is my goal for us, with every word I share. That is what I want for myself, my family, and you, too, dear reader.

I want us to be excited about our lives, to know our beautiful purpose without questioning our goals. I know this is a lot to hope for, so I seek God's word and direction. There is nothing our Heavenly Father cannot do for His children, His followers, and His creation. For that is who we are to Him, and so much more.

Many of us face daily challenges in our lives, and it can become difficult to keep moving forward. But no matter what you may be going through or facing, always know that God is never far away from you. We therefore must neither give up nor give in.

We must never stop making progress. We must stand strong together in our faith and continue to believe in a better tomorrow. In light of that, we must remember all of God's blessings and all of His promises. New blessings are coming our way every day.

Continued

As a beloved child of God, dear reader, you have no need to stress, worry, or lose sleep. You can walk through life confidently and courageously and know that life will be okay as long as you continue to trust, believe, and have faith. With that I invite you to join us on a loving journey of faith, peace, and tranquility. Come see, hear and feel life through the thoughts of a poet's heart and mind.

God's Guiding Light of Peace

A Note from the Author

I fell in love with reading, writing, and poetry in the second grade. That little girl's love of poetry continues to live in my heart every day. After my eye injuries and visual impairment, I went into a deep spiral of loss, pain, fear, hurt, and anger.

When I was at the worst point in my life, and walking through a dark valley, I started writing, and light returned to my world. Writing allows me to understand life's changes and to fight the chronic eye pain I live with.

I shared some of my poetry and inspirational thoughts with my family and close friends. My father took ill and shared his dream of me publishing a book. So I took some of my best pieces, and with the help of a great team we published my first poetry and essay collection.

We are now five books into a wonderful inspirational series, *Poetry from the Heart*. God has taken all of my broken pieces and turned them into a message and a blessing through the medium of poetry.

I hope you will take the time to check out the other volumes in our *Poetry from the Heart Collection* and purchase a book for yourself and someone that you love.

Please enjoy the next step of our journey to peace.

God's Guiding Light of Peace

Introduction

Each day I attempt to be the best servant of God that I know how to be. As a child of God, I believe that part of my life's journey is to continue to gain knowledge and grow my understanding of God's desires. I believe that part of my life's purpose, journey and responsibility is to help others on their path to a more inspired, fulfilling life.

I do not physically get out and meet a lot of new people, though I often interact with God's children in various other ways. I may receive a phone call, a text, or an email. However, I connect with the person I seek to find a way to be of help or at least bring a smile to that person's day.

Often I intuitively sense a lesson in the occurrence. Sometimes it is a friend of a friend, or a friend of a family member, who wants or needs my advice. Other times they are total strangers.

As our paths cross, and an opportunity to assist becomes clear, my spirit is touched, my hand is directed, and I receive God's grace to be able to help. However God sends them to me, I always appreciate His divine instruction. Sometimes it is I who receives the lesson. What I find is that answers come to me, thoughts pour out of my heart, and lives are enhanced.

It is my hope that someone has come into your life and helped you find your way to the path of your purpose. There is no greater joy than choosing to walk entirely in your God-given purpose. Whether or not you feel you have found your purpose, I wish you well on your journey.

God's Guiding Light of Peace

Continued

Make proactive choices to improve the quality of your health, your heart, your mind, and your life. Be better, stronger, wiser, and love more than you ever have before. Know that you are more than enough to make your dreams come true. God loves you, for He is the Creator of love, and His love always surrounds you and is never far away from you.

I want you to remain encouraged and to continue standing firm through the storms life will send your way. You are well equipped and able to survive! We serve a mighty God. God is always good, and He is always faithful.

The enemy of our souls is always busy, though he will never prevail. God has already promised our victory! Trust and believe that God is always in your corner, standing with you and fighting for you. As long as you have faith in your heart and mind, you will never be alone.

Collection Focus Scripture:
*If you look for Me wholeheartedly,
you will find Me.*
— *Jeremiah 29:13 (NLT)*

God's Guiding Light of Peace

Rest in God's Tranquility

May your heart be happy
And your mind be worry-free.
May you always feel the love
Of God surrounding you.
May you always find comfort
And rest in His peace and tranquility.

God's Guiding Light of Peace

Contents

Preface
A Note from the Author
Introduction
Collection Focus Scripture: Jeremiah 29:13 (NLT)
Poem: Rest in God's Tranquility

Opening Prayer: We Pray and Give Thanks 1

Chapter 1: Embracing God's Strength 3
Thoughts and Reflections
Focus Scripture: 1 John 3:1a 3

Essays of Thought:
The Strength We Have 4
My Morning with God 5
Give Yourself a Break 6

Poetry Messages of God's Love:
Listen to Me 7
Fully Trust Me 8
Practice What You Preach 9
Focus and Breathe 10
There is Hope for You 11

Essays of Thought:
God's Response in My Heart:
Extend Your Compassion to You 12
Dear Heavenly Father 13
You Know What You Must Do 14
My Heart Speaking the Dream 15
I Communicate in Many Ways 16-17

Contents

Chapter 2: Embracing Our Daily Blessings 19
Live Mindfully and Make Intentional Steps
Focus Scripture: Psalms 1:3 (KJV) 19

Essays of Thought:
My Heart's Response 20
God's Response in My Heart:
You, My Love, Are Part of My Light 21-22
Find Moments of Silence, Serenity, and Peace 23

Poetry Messages of God's Love:
My Beautiful Child 24
My Grace 25
Trust Me 26
Guard Your Peace 27
Leave Your Troubles with Me 28
Keep Focused on My Peace 29
Place Your Focus on Me 30
My Unwavering Hand 31
Send Me Your Worry and Fear 32
The Path to Everlasting Life 33
Embrace Your Strengths 34
Love's Creator 35
My Ever-Loving Grace 36
I Send You My Blessings 37
See Through Eyes of Faith 38
You Are Always Enough 39

Contents

Chapter 3: Embracing the Full Beauty of Life 41
Focus Scripture: Jeremiah 29:11 (NIV)..................41

Essay of Thought:
Reflecting the Best 42-43

Poetry Messages of God's Love:
Happiness is Meant for You 44
You Will Never Be Alone 45
Baby, You Are My Star 46

Poem of Reflection:
Peace During your Storm 47

Recommended Scriptures:
Finding Strength in God's Word
What the Bible Tells Us About Peace 48
What the Bible Tells Us About God's Promises 49
What the Bible Tells Us About God's Love 50

Note to Reader:
Just Breathe 51

Essays of Thought:
What God Has Said in My Heart:
Be Mindful, Remain Obedient 52
Trusting the Calm 53
What God Has Said in My Heart:
I Will Keep You Safe 54

Poem: God's Love 55

Contents

Chapter 4: Life Will Be Ok 57
Leaning on God for Comfort
Focus Scripture: Exodus 15:2 (NLT) 57

My Prayer Responses:
Father God 58
I am Crying Out to You 59

Poetic Reflections:
What God Said in My Heart:
Walk Through Life in My Peace 60
Who You Are in My Eyes 61
Father, See Me Through 62
Trust My Holy Spirit 63
My Thoughts 64
God's Response in My Heart:
I Love You 64
You Are Covered in My Grace 65
My Sweet Embrace 66
Life Will Be Okay 67
Share My Truth and My Light 68
Trust in My Sufficiency 69
Remain Zealous and Seek Me 70
Live in My Peace 71
Believe in Your Breakthrough 72
My Response and Commitment 73
God's Response in My Heart:
My Power Lives in You 74

Essay of Thought:
Listen to My Spirit and My Direction 75

Contents

Chapter 5: The Joy of the Lord is Our Strength 77
Stay on the Right Path to Truth and Light
Focus Scripture: Psalms 118:14 (KJV)....................77

Poetic Reflections:
Fill Me Up 78
Thank You for My Journey 79
God Cares for Us 80
My Words Bring Comfort 81
You Are Covered in My Love 82
A Well-Lived Life 83

Empowering Affirmations:
An Affirmation of Being 84
An Affirmation of Balance 84
An Affirmation of Worth 84
An Affirmation of Peaceful Living 85
An Affirmation of Acceptance 85
An Affirmation of Purpose 85
An Affirmation of Gratitude 86
An Affirmation of Happiness 86
An Affirmation of Joy 86
An Affirmation of New Beginnings 87
An Affirmation of Life 87
Your Personal Affirmation 87

Poem: God is Sending What You Need 88

Essay of Thought:
Every Day is a Sweet Blessing 89-90

Contents

Chapter 5 Continued

Tips to Live Happier: 91

Closing Thoughts:
Choose to Walk in a Spirit of Gratitude 92

Summary of Thoughts: 93

Closing Prayer:
You Are Worthy of Our Praise...................................95

Afterword...96

Dedication 97

About the Author 101

Other Books By C. Melita Webb 103

God's Guiding Light of Peace

God's Guiding Light of Peace

God's Guiding Light of Peace

Opening Prayer:
We Pray and Give Thanks

Father God,
We thank You for every ounce
Of Your daily grace
And for every moment
Of Your divine favor.
We appreciate the way You make
The sun rise each morning
And the moon glow for us every night.
Father, we enjoy every drop
Of the cleansing rain.
We appreciate the fresh morning dew
You make appear at dawn
And the refreshing wind
You cause to blow our way.
Father, we do not take
Any of Your loving gifts,
Your redeeming grace,
Or Your sweet blessings for granted.
We know that every good thing
Comes from You.
Father, we love You and cherish
All of Your sweet and divine designs.
We pray and give thanks to You for
Your continued blessings and favor.

God's Guiding Light of Peace

God's Guiding Light of Peace

Chapter 1:
Embracing God's Strength

Thoughts and reflections of standing through the storm.

Focus Scripture:

See what great love the Father has lavished on us, that we should be called children of God! And that is what we are!
— 1 John 3:1a

Essays of Thought: The Strength We Have

There is a strength we have in life that many of us do not always fully embrace. During life's challenges, changes and difficulties, we can feel lost or alone, because we spend so much time trying to figure out our next step.

For me, faith is my next step. My faith in God helps me stand and find my way during and through adversity. My trust in God gives me hope and helps me believe in a better tomorrow. Because of my faith, I know we can all be friends and help each other build better communities.

Life does not come with an instruction book, though it does come with a guide. May we all rely more on our faith and less on our worries. Hold on to your faith and stand firm.

My Morning with God

You are having problems because you are not listening to Me. I have made you strong, and I have made you free. I have released you from your past, and I have shown you how to remove all of your enemies. You remain confused. Why, when I am the only one you need? I am the only one who can help your mind be free. Focus on My word, and truly listen to Me.

I did not call you to be used, abused, confused, or mistreated. I called you to bless, to love, and to praise My holy name. Think about what keeps you and your heart from Me. That is the thorn in your eye, and it is what prevents you from fully seeing Me work within your life and truly connecting with Me.

You were correct when you said you are only the mother of two. You cannot raise grown people. Continue to extend your loving kindness to others. If they refuse, let them be. That means they are content existing without Me. For if they were walking with Me, you would know it. Their actions would show it. Release them, and let them come back to Me.

You cannot save those who choose not to seek and embrace My Spirit, nor should you continue to try. I have called you to save hundreds and thousands with the words I am giving to you. I have already shown you how it could end. Release them when you see that they are not with Me. Through your heart, you have found Me. I have now called you direct, and I have made you free.

Give Yourself a Break

You may be going through something difficult right now, and you may not know which path is the correct one to take. I want to encourage you to not give up hope, and to give yourself a break.

We have a tendency to rush through life, especially when we are younger. As we grow in age, years and wisdom, we learn to slow down. Even then, we must remind ourselves to be more mindful and assess what is truly going on with us before we make important decisions.

So give yourself permission to take the time you need to care for yourself. Take time to breathe deep, clear your thoughts, and get some fresh air. Then make the best decision you are able to make, to be sure that what you are doing will give you the best outcome.

Even when I am filled with doubt, I know who knows the answers to my every need. I want to encourage you to trust God and to lean on Him for understanding.

Find calm, peace, and comfort in your restful nights. Wake up refreshed to the morning light. Start each day with your mind worry-free.

Poetry Messages of God's Love:
Listen to Me

Keep moving forward
And continue progressing daily
In your journey with Me.
If you truly believe,
Stop holding on to the negativity.
Accept your God-given release.
I have removed your chains,
And I have already set you free.
I have spoken directly to you.
Stop, hear all of My words,
And truly listen to Me.

Fully Trust Me

Why is it that you
Do not fully trust Me?
Release this world's hold,
Come closer, and show Me
That you truly believe.
I am sending you signs,
Placing words within your heart
And covering you with My favor.
You must remain open to receiving
My lessons and My blessings
And choosing to look
For the deeper meaning within them.
If and when you do,
You will see some of
My greatest blessings
Unfold for you.

God's Guiding Light of Peace

Practice What You Preach

You may believe
That you are not a preacher,
Though you must accept
And build upon
What I have placed
Inside of you.
The encouraging words
You share are Mine.
I have given them to you.
You speak only for My glory.
You must walk, listen, learn,
And live for My glory too.
Your life is precious,
And this is a wake-up call.

Focus and Breathe

Take a few deep breaths.
Really focus yourself
And just breathe.
Give yourself a break.
Think about what you need.
You must remain focused
To keep hearing from Me.
Rely on My word for your knowledge
And speak My truth for power.
Smile, trust, and continue to believe
That I am taking care
Of all your needs.

There is Hope for You

If you can feel the warmth
Of the rising sun,
There is hope for you
Wherever you come from.
If you can hear, see or smell
The beauty of the rain,
You can learn to enjoy
Your life again.
If you can enjoy the feeling
Of grass underneath your feet,
You can open your heart
And find the happiness you seek.

With God there is always hope.

God's Guiding Light of Peace

Essays of Thought:
God's Response in My Heart:
Extend Your Compassion to You

Your compassion can occasionally go a little too far. As My beloved child, you are designed in My image, and I understand your desire to help. However, you cannot truly help someone who does not want to accept your help. You must learn to be compassionate for yourself, too.

You can only save someone for a minute. Offer them what you know is the information and assistance they need. Then look at how they choose to react. They are responsible for their choices. They must be willing to grab hold of their life and plan for their future. Sometimes the people you love the most can, will and do take you for granted.

I will cause My strength and power to work with the universe to give you what you need once you decide to move. You must be willing to still your body and calm your mind. I am your God, and I am talking to you. Stop, be silent, be still, and listen. For I have not called you to suffer. I have called you to peace. You will only suffer when you do not listen to Me.

God's Guiding Light of Peace

Dear Heavenly Father

    I thank You for all of the goodness You bless me with each day. Please continue speaking to me and through me. My mind can sometimes become distracted, full of anxiety, worry and fear. It is then that I closely search my heart and my mind to find Your words for comfort.

    Father, I know and I believe Your spirit is always near. Knowing of your constant presence provides me with great comfort and alleviates many of my fears. I am ashamed to admit, however, that I do not know all of the verses by heart.

    Father, I am doing my best to be a good student, to listen intently for Your spirit, and to willingly receive all lessons You send to me. I often fall short, and I fear that my actions may be going against You.

    Father, I am thankful that, even when I do not have the words to tell You my concerns, You still know my heart. I have no desire to go against Your will.
I earnestly seek each day to be a better servant to You. Father, please help me be more mindful. Teach me how to better listen to You.

God's Response in My Heart: You Know What You Must Do

My beloved child, you already know what you must do. Stop when you hear My Holy Spirit speak to you. It may not be My voice, though I am sending you My thoughts. You know how best to do what I have called you to do.

I have made ways for you to receive everything you need. The technology, the medicine you take that helps you continue to live, breathe and see, the breathing machines—all of that was from Me. Yet you continue to walk in fear. What more do I need to say, for you to be able to hear?

Even in your trials, I continue to give you My grace. Your path may not always be smooth, straight, easy, or clear, but you, My dear, have made it halfway through. Now it will be up to you to listen closely and do what I say you must do.

Each day of your life is filled with wonderful opportunities for joy. Life meets you where you are and waits for you to make the next step. Choose to reach for what you want most, and understand that any battle you may face is already won. Continue to build daily on your faith, and enjoy all of the smiles I send your way.

God's Guiding Light of Peace

My Heart Speaking the Dream

Father, I will do what You tell me to do. Sometimes I get the message You graciously send loud and clear. Other times I fail to understand the message I believe is sent from You. I know it is my human condition that fogs my mind and brings distractions that always seem to be near.

I thought You wanted me to write a book, *Step into Your Destiny*. It was in my dream. I was walking into a room, I saw the signs on the wall behind the podium and they seemed to be clear: A Talk *Step into Your Destiny*, by *C. Melita Webb*. Now, many months later, I read a book by that title published by another faithful servant of You. I must ask You, Father, what do I need to do?

God has more goodness planned for you.

~15~

God's Response in My Heart: I Communicate in Many Ways

That dream was Me. I was showing you one way your destiny could lead you. There is much more for Me to do with you, and many ways that dream may still come true. Your path is always clear to Me, though I know you have a different view.

Trust Me, and continue to walk in My ways. My words are what you must hold onto. Any time you feel confused about My communication with you, return to Me in prayer. Trust and believe that My directions to you will always accord with My Word. Some things may have a different meaning to you. What should be clear is that I am always near, and I have more goodness planned for you. Your path is clear, and your future is bright, though only if you continue to stand in My Light.

In man's world, you will continue to be in darkness, though that is not My final plan for your life. With Me, you will always be in the light. After all, you are My child created, loved and anointed for My purpose, so I will always protect you.

Return to your path, and plan to enjoy your journey. Do not become anxious, for anxiety does not originate with Me. Do not react out of anger, for anger, too, is against My spirit. I need you to stand strong and to maintain your faith and focus.

Continued

    Stop worrying and lingering in earthly fears. Keep your spirit tuned into My word, My wishes, My desire, and My glory. That is what is best for you.

    You have free will, therefore the choice is always yours. You must decide what you will do. My heart remains open, and with Me, there is always a special place for you.

    Focus on the Fruits of the Spirit. These are the thoughts that must live in you:

> *"But the fruit of the Spirit is love, joy, peace, patience, kindness, goodness, faithfulness, gentleness, and self-control."*
> *— Galatians 5:22-23 (Berean Study Bible)*

Chapter 2:
Embracing Our Daily Blessings

Live mindfully, and make intentional steps.
Continue to place your mind and trust in Jesus.

Focus Scripture:

And he shall be like a tree planted by the rivers of water, that bringeth forth his fruit in his season; his leaf also shall not wither; and whatsoever he doeth shall prosper.
— *Psalms 1:3 (KJV)*

Essays of Thought:
My Heart's Response

Father, I choose You. I will always choose You. Sometimes I become anxious, and I try to move even closer to You. I try to pray, meditate, and fight the spirits of anxiety, depression and fear. Often, it is my fear that brings the spirits of anxiety and depression near.

You will always be a beloved child of God.

God's Response in My Heart: You, My Love, Are Part of My Light

Welcome each new day with joy and enthusiasm. You must trust that all you need will be provided and all things are aligned for your good. Focus on the blessings and positivity I continue to place in your life.

You, My love, are part of My light. The world's darkness cannot touch or control you unless you give in to sin. Continue to harness your strengths and shine your light bright. You are strong, wise, powerful, and unique. You are everything I created you to be. You have the ability and free will to set the tone for your life. So choose to walk each day in the way that brings you the most peace.

There are many spirits, just as there are many stars. Some spirits are positive; others are negative. Understand that any feelings you have that do not align with the goodness in My word are against Me and your best interest. It is up to you to recognize the spirits' presence. Once you realize something is against My wishes, choose to fully pull back your mind and emotions.

You cannot afford to be lukewarm, neither hot nor cold, regarding My word. You have come too far, seen too much, and known too much of My truth to be indecisive. I can protect you only if you are fully Mine. Each choice you make is up to you. Take your time, and choose your steps with care.

Continued

    Stop all worry at the first sign that it is trying to come into your mind. It is then, My child, that you must pray without haste. Pray, and I will send My Spirit to drape and cover you. Fear must not be allowed to get anywhere near.

    When gloom, doom and negativity reach out and touch you, you must stand firm and say, "Negativity be gone. Flee from me. This is not where you belong. I am the beloved and honored child of the Most High God, and I am never alone."

    My child, whenever you need Me, just call out My name, and My spirit will be there. You will not see My hands move, though they are always working positively for you. Trust in My words, and I will continue to guide you. Allow My grace to prepare you for the next step in your journey.

    Keep your eyes and ears open, and you will continue to receive My mercy and My grace. For I am always sending tender blessings and new goodness your way.

Find Moments of Silence, Serenity, and Peace

It is important to the quality of your life and mental health to find moments of silence, serenity and peace. The calming quality of silence allows you to refresh your mind, rest your body, and rejuvenate your spirit. The comforting quality of serenity and peace will remind you of God's presence. You can find more balance in your life and increase the clarity of your mind in the quiet beauty of peace.

Treasure your silence, serenity, and peace.

God's Guiding Light of Peace

Poetry Messages of God's Love: My Beautiful Child

My beautiful child,
Come closer to Me
And sit here
In My presence.
Many of the loads you often choose
Are not yours alone to carry.
Release to Me
What causes you stress,
Difficulties or pain.
Leave those concerns at My feet.
Pray, seek My peace
And request My assistance.
You will always find Me near.
Continue to do the best
That you can do.
Reflect My love and My light.
Beloved, You have My word,
You will be all right.

My Grace

Hold on, My blessed
And beloved child.
My grace is clearing
A path for you.
Remain steadfast,
Faithful and true.
Stand firm in all
I have called you to do.

Trust Me

Continue to believe
And trust Me.
Place My words
Into the deepest parts
Of your heart.
You will have great comfort
While living in My light.
Know that,
Beyond today's challenges
Are tomorrow's victories.

God's Guiding Light of Peace

Guard Your Peace

Choose to live your life
In full acceptance of My peace.
With My peace you will be surrounded
By positivity and complete harmony.
Let nothing and no one disturb
What I have set aside for you.
Hold firmly to your inner peace
And guard your place of serenity.
Visualize your heart's
Sweetest desires coming true.
Believe in your destiny,
And know that goodness
Is meant for you.

Leave Your Troubles with Me

Forget about what troubles you,
As those are the things
You need to leave with Me.
Release your problems.
Choose to set your heart
And your soul free.
Keep focused on My joy,
And continue to invite
My essence to surround you.
With My joy
Is calm, love, peace,
And tranquility.
Even when you feel
You are at your worst,
Know that I am
Sending you My best.
I will always work things out
For your victory.

God's Guiding Light of Peace

Keep Focused on My Peace

If you find yourself in conflict,
Stop and think of peace.
Step back from adversity.
Refuse to be a part
Of the world's problems.
Refocus yourself on My peace.
Reclaim the calmness in your mind,
And rebuke all negativity.
Call out to Me.
Withdraw from all conflict.
Find the center of your balance.
There you will find My comfort
And your path to My unyielding peace.

God's Guiding Light of Peace

Place Your Focus on Me

My anointed child,
Step back and cast away
All of your anxiety.
Bring your focus back to Me.
Release all of your worries.
Put down and leave behind
All of your grief.
Walk away from your sadness,
And the sorrow will be released.
I can ease your troubles,
And I can make your blues go away.
Your faithful path is covered in My love,
And your way is paved in My grace.

God's Guiding Light of Peace

My Unwavering Hand

I am here whenever
You have a need.
I will always lend My ear,
And I will calm your life
With My unwavering hand.
I will stand with you
In the burning sun.
I will fight with you against
The strongest winds
And the highest waves.
I will shelter you
From the hardest rain.
Fully place your trust in Me,
And allow your mind to find
My perfect joy again.

God's Guiding Light of Peace

Send Me Your Worry and Fear

Precious child of God,
Rise and meet the new day.
Be thankful for
The morning sun,
The afternoon rain,
And the cool evening breeze.
I, your Heavenly Father,
Am taking care
Of all your needs.
If anxiety, stress, or fear
Attempt to come near,
Block them from your mind.
Send your worries
To Me in prayer.
Do not get caught up
In worldly distractions.
Be Christ-like
In all of your actions.

God's Guiding Light of Peace

The Path to Everlasting Life

Send Me Your Worry and Fear
Stay on the righteous
Path of My truth,
And continue to walk in My light.
The road to peace is narrow,
Though the pathway is bright.
It is I and My Holy Spirit
That will lead you to everlasting life.
My words are always true,
And My ways are always right.
Count on Me to assist you,
And never willingly dim your light.

Embrace Your Strengths

I find delight in all
Of the good things you do.
No longer question
If I am genuinely
Communicating with you.
Continue to build on your faith,
And I will continue to be with you.
Be confident in your journey,
Embrace your strengths,
And you will find more
Of My peace and My light.

Love's Creator

As the Creator of love,
I have dispatched My love
To completely cover you.
There is no fear in My love,
Nor should there be
Any fear in you.
Decry the spirit of fear,
Keep your heart full of faith,
And you will feel the full presence
Of My warmth and My embrace.

My Ever-Loving Grace

Take some time each day
To rest, reflect and pray.
Choose to be embraced
By My life-giving words
And My ever-loving grace.
There is strength found in silence
And calm found in peace.
Honor Me and yourself
With the quiet time you need.
Relax and rejuvenate with Me.
Your soul is worthy of My peace.
Understand that the true beauty
Of life is often found
In quiet moments of simplicity.

God's Guiding Light of Peace

I Send You My Blessings

Each day I send you My blessings
To match with your faith.
When you take time
And send Me your prayers,
I send even more of My love
And My strength there.
When you search the depth
Of your heart for loving words
And you choose to pray,
My Holy Spirit draws nearer to you
Each and every day.

See Through Eyes of Faith

My thoughtful Child,
Search your heart
And look deep within.
There are many gifts
I have blessed you with
That are unique to you.
You are a part
Of My greatest treasure.
Embrace your eyes of faith
To envision My plans for you.
Keep true to My word,
And My gifts
Will remain with you.

God's Guiding Light of Peace

You Are Always Enough

You are a walking miracle,
A wonderful blessing,
And a beautiful tribute to Me.
You have many talents
You have yet to discover.
Trust that your peace will recover.
Look deep within and believe
In all you are in Me.
You are always enough.
You were anointed at birth
To fulfill your purpose
And reach your dreams.

God's Guiding Light of Peace

Chapter 3:
Embracing the Full Beauty of Life

There is a new layer of joy in your life
When you feel the love of God growing in your heart.

Focus Scripture:

'I Know the plans I have for you,' declares the Lord, 'plans to prosper you and not to harm you, plans to give you hope and a future.'
— Jeremiah 29:11 (NIV)

Essay of Thought: Reflecting the Best

Choose to reflect only the best, for that is what I have placed inside of you. My beloved one, hold onto the goodness I have bestowed upon you. I have planned all of your steps and designed your destiny; It is up to you to become who I know you can be. I designed your being at the time I created the universe.

You are always in My thoughts. From the first breath I blew into your nostrils to fill your lungs and bring life to you, I have cared for you. I always know what it is that you need. Nothing can touch you unless I say so.

I call you to remain faithful to Me and stay true to what I have placed into your heart. I created you to stand strong, and that is certainly what you will do. Continue to build on your faith, and embrace all of the blessings I send to you.

Choose to accentuate the best parts of your life. Be mindful, and do not flee into stress or willingly seek situations of strife. Pray about what concerns you and that which you know needs to be released. Only you can choose to set your mind and your soul free. Remember, I make sure that all things are working out for your good.

Go to My word, call out to Me, or seek My counsel in prayer whenever your mind tries to lead you into troubled waters. Do not rush out to meet the storms, face the bellowing winds, or run into the torrent rains. Instead, rest your burdens on My shoulders. Lay down what pains you at My feet. Know that I will always cover you with My love.

God's Guiding Light of Peace

Continued

    You may feel sick, and you may even grow tired and become weary. My child, I promise you, you will not be defeated. With Me, you will always be safe. I will see to your every need, and I have assured your victory. My child, you are faithful and true. Why would you think I have anything but goodness in store for you?

    My children are always under My protection. Under this world's system of things, storms will keep coming, and you must remain standing. As My beloved child, you may wobble, and you may occasionally stumble. Understand that I will always strengthen you. I will help you rise and continue to stand.

    I want to encourage you to continue to reinforce your faith and stand firm against the storms that will come your way. I have made you strong and equipped you well, so you will be able to survive.

    Always be thankful for your life and embrace every day, as each day is a blessing from Me. Even in times of difficulties, you can find comfort by choosing to recognize life's beauty and your life's blessings.

Poetry Messages of God's Love
Happiness is Meant for You

See humanity through eyes of love.
Embrace all of My children with care.
Do not settle for less
Than you are worth.
Joy is your right,
Peace is your right,
Respect is your right,
And happiness is meant for you.
The way to joy
Is to accept My love.
The way to peace
Is to accept My direction,
And always choose
To embrace My grace.

God's Guiding Light of Peace

You Will Never Be Alone

I am God Almighty.
I am always good,
And I am always faithful.
The enemy of your soul
Is always busy,
Though he will never prevail,
For I have made a way for you.
Continue to follow My words
And march strong toward your victory!
Trust and believe
I am always standing
In your corner
And fighting for you.
As long as you have faith,
You will never be alone.

Baby, You Are My Star

Life can occasionally become confusing,
Difficult to manage, and sometimes
Things may dampen your spirits.
Hold onto My love, and never forget
That you are one of My shining stars.
Baby, I will love you forever.
There is nothing that you can do
That will block, prevent or stop
Me from loving you.

Nothing can stop God from loving you.

Poem of Reflection:
Peace During Your Storm

You will find peace
During your storm.
Know in your heart
That you will be okay.
Trust that I,
Your Heavenly Father,
Will always make a way.
Stand strong
And be prepared
To carry on.
I am with you,
Even in the midst
Of your storm.
Believe that I am bringing
My relief to you.
Keep calm, and trust Me
In all you do.

God's Guiding Light of Peace

Recommended Scriptures: Finding Strength in God's Word

What the Bible Tells Us About Peace

Peacemakers who sow in peace reap a harvest of righteousness.
— James 3:18 (NIV)

And the peace, which transcends all understanding, will guard your hearts and your minds in Christ Jesus.
— Philippians 4:7 (NIV)

The Lord gives strength to His people; the Lord blesses His people with peace.
— Psalms 29:11 (NIV)

Peace I leave with you; My peace I give you. I do not give to you as the world gives. Do not let your hearts be troubled and do not be afraid.
— John 14:27 (NIV)

Praise the Lord! Happy are those who fear the Lord. They are not afraid of evil tidings; their hearts are firm, secure in the Lord. Their hearts are steady, they will not be afraid.
— Psalm 112:1,7-8 (NRSB)

You will keep in perfect peace those whose minds are steadfast, because they trust in You.
— Isaiah 26:3 (NIV)

What the Bible Tells Us About God's Promises

So do not fear, for I am with you; do not be dismayed, for I am your God. I will strengthen you and help you; I will uphold you with My righteous right hand.
— *Isaiah 41:10 (NIV)*

The LORD Himself goes before you and will be with you; He will never leave you nor forsake you. Do not be afraid; do not be discouraged.
— *Deuteronomy 31:8 (NIV)*

The Lord will fight for you; you only need to be still.
—*Ephesians 14:14 (NIV)*

He gives strength to the weary and increases the power of the weak.
— *Isaiah 40:29 (NIV)*

9 The Lord is a refuge for the oppressed, a stronghold in times of trouble. 10 Those who know Your name trust in You, for You, Lord, have never forsaken those who seek You.
— *Psalm 9:9-10 (NIV)*

2 Praise the Lord, my soul, and forget not all His benefits- 3 who forgives all your sins and heals all your diseases, 4 who redeems your life from the pit and crowns you with love and compassion, 5 who satisfies your desires with good things so that your youth is renewed like the eagle's.
—*Psalm 103:2-5 (NIV)*

What the Bible Tells Us About God's Love

Let all bitterness and wrath and anger and clamor and slander be put away from you, along with all malice. Be kind to one another, tenderhearted, forgiving one another, as God in Christ forgave you.
— *Ephesians 4:31-32 (ESV)*

For God hath not given us the spirit of fear; but of power, and of love, and of a sound mind.
— *2 Timothy 1:7 (NIV)*

13 Then they cried to the Lord in their trouble's, and He saved them from their distress. 14 He brought them out of darkness, the utter darkness, and broke away their chains. 15 Let them give thanks to the Lord for His unfailing love and His wonderful deeds for mankind, 16 for he breaks down gates of bronze and cuts through bars of iron.
—*Psalm 107:13-16 (NIV)*

16 I pray that out of his glorious riches he may strengthen you with power through his Spirit in your inner being, 17 so that Christ may dwell in your hearts through faith. And I pray that you, being rooted and established in love, 18 may have power, together with all the Lord's holy people, to grasp how wide and long and high and deep is the love of Christ, 19 and to know this love that surpasses knowledge—that you may be filled to the measure of all the fullness of God.
—*Ephesians 3:16-19 (NIV*

God's Guiding Light of Peace

A Note to the Reader:
Just Breathe

Please take a few moments to close your eyes and just breathe. Think about the peace you seek and the peace that you need. Allow God's love to sink deeper in your heart. Use God's love to find your balance and your peace again.

Breathe, pray, and allow God to intercede.

Essays of Thought:
What God Has Said in My Heart:
Be Mindful, Remain Obedient

What I believe this means, and so it is, that peace will continue to make its way into you, and flow out to others because of you. That is My will, My wish, and My plan.

Things may not always appear to be going your way. You must remain flexible as you walk your life's pathto reach the destination I have planned for you.

Some days you have to be willing to see the beauty in the rain. Hold on, and the storm will pass. Then the sun will rise, and it will shine again. Continue to lean on My words as you walk through your day. I am sending you signs and messages that will take your troubles, your blues, and your fears away.

If you are not mindful, you are not being obedient to Me. When you allow Me to communicate with you, I can speak through you and use your issues to help others who also are looking for peace in their storms and calm on their paths.

Trusting the Calm

I was reminded by life circumstance that things could change in a moment. We never truly know what will happen any second before it happens. Unexpected things will occur, and we will need to make adjustments to continue forward in our journeys.

What is reassuring is that, when we store up goodness in our hearts and minds, we will receive that goodness back in many ways. Often that goodness is returned as a calmness—sort of an intuitive trust that, whatever I face, I will not be alone.

That calmness allowed me to remain in an aware, thoughtful state, without undue stress or anxiety. It does not mean I did not have any concern. I just had the presence of mind to tread lightly and decide to gather all of the facts before choosing to react.

What God Has Said in My Heart:
I Will Keep You Safe

Choose to listen when I speak. Be present in your mind at all times. Allowing stress and daily life challenges to keep your mind cluttered will block your ability to hear Me. Trust that I am always in communication with you. Even in your sleep, My spirit is there beside you, calming any storms that seek to disturb you.

The enemy is strong. I promise you, I am stronger. He can ruffle the water and make waves. My dear, it is I who formed the waters, created the wind, and designed the rain. I have the final say. I will always calm your waters and return them to a peaceful state. Lean fully on Me as you walk, sleep, eat and pray. Do not cut Me out of any part of your day. It is I who will keep you safe.

God will keep you safe.

God's Love

You are not lost,
Forgotten, or alone.
You forever remain
Precious in God's eyes.
God will always
Be with you,
And every day
He holds you dearly
In His heart.
God's love
Knows no bounds,
No barriers and no limits.
He will never stop loving you.

Chapter 4:
Life Will Be Okay
Leaning on God for comfort.

Focus Scripture:
*The Lord is my strength and my song; He has given me victory.
This is my God, and I will praise Him,
my father's God, and I will exalt Him!
— Exodus 15: 2 (NLT)*

My Response

Thank you, Father. I am listening,
And I am obeying.

My Prayerful Reflections: Father God

Father God,
Only You know what it is
That I am truly going through.
You saw the storm coming
Before the wind began to move.
You heard the whispers in the clouds
Before I felt the first raindrop.
Father, nothing can happen
Without Your knowledge
And Your will.
Please continue to be with me
And shelter me, Father,
From the storms at hand.
With You,
I know I will be all right.

God's Guiding Light of Peace

I Am Crying Out to You

Father, my heart and my soul
Are crying out to You.
I am only able to remain standing,
Because I totally trust
And believe in You.
Father, You see the end
Before the beginning.
You can fix any problem
Before it starts.
So, Father, I am giving all
Of my troubles to You.
Father, I am freeing up my heart,
Clearing the troubles
Out of my mind,
And I am allowing my spirit
To rest calmly with You.

God's Guiding Light of Peace

What God Said in My Heart: Walk Through Life in My Peace

Good, now let Me expel all of your fears.
Trust Me when I say:
My perfect peace will always cover you.
My infinite power will always protect you.
My amazing grace will always lead your way.
My love will always overcome hate.
My light will always drive out the darkness.
Walking through life in My peace
Will always be the best choice.
And, most importantly,
Doing My will ensures your future with Me.
I will never leave your side or abandon you.

Who You Are in My Eyes

When I look at you,
I see the beauty only I can create.
I see your heart.
I hear your thoughts.
I feel your soul.
I know your ways.
I will always see the best in you.
As My beloved child,
You are kept here, with Me
And tucked safely in My heart.

God's Guiding Light of Peace

Father, See Me Through

Thank you for protecting me, Father.
Thank you for seeing me through.
I know You always hear
The words in my mind.
I know Your spirit
Is with me all the time.
Thank you for protecting me
And for seeing me through.
Father, my life gets brighter
Every day because of You!

Trust My Holy Spirit

Trust My Holy Spirit.
Walk in peace and listen
Fully to My spirit.
Slow down, center yourself,
And decide to be mindful.
Trust that My Holy Spirit
Is sending you inspiration
And information.

My Thoughts

Dear Father,
I always find comfort
In Your majestic presence.
I thank you for Your daily grace.

God's Response:
I Love You

I love you, and I always will.
It does not matter how you look,
What you think, or how you feel.
Nothing can stop My love
From reaching you.
You are My beloved
Whom I have called and approved.
Nothing can turn
My love away from you.
To Me, you are more precious
Than diamonds, rubies, and pearls.
There is nothing
More valuable than you.

God's Guiding Light of Peace

You Are Covered in My Grace

Focus on the many blessings
That you receive each day.
Doing so will help send
Your stress and blues away.
Lean fully into My presence
And become more covered in My grace.
Choose to be embraced by My love
And to continue growing stronger in faith.
In My eyes, nothing can dim your light.
I will always keep My covenant with you.

My Sweet Embrace

I send you beautiful messages
Of love every day.
Be sure to take time
To send a loving message
Back My way.
Look up, reach out,
And enjoy My sweet embrace.
Rest fully in the comfort
Of My Holy Spirit.
Allow Me to mend, restore
And complete you.

Life Will Be Okay

Trust that life will be okay.
Breathe deep, say a prayer,
And send your worries away.
Keep peace and positivity
Forefront in your mind;
You will feel more hope,
And joy will flow freely
In your heart all the time.
No matter what hardships you face,
Will go through,
Or have been through,
You remain a blessed miracle.
You are a beautiful child of God.
Your life matters,
And your birth was important.
So you must trust
That life will be okay.

God's Guiding Light of Peace

Share My Truth and My Light

I am always thinking of you,
Caring for you,
And preparing for you.
I delight in all of your joys
And in your happiness, too.
I am pleased when you
Follow My word.
Seeing you choose to live right
And share the joy in your life
Will help others find their path
To My truth and My light

God's Guiding Light of Peace

Trust in My Sufficiency

Dear one, trust Me
With your whole being.
Lay open your heart,
Bare your soul,
And expand your mind.
Fully surrender to Me.
Warmly welcome
All of My love
Into your heart.
Find safety and rest
In My sufficiency
And live under
My loving care.

God's Guiding Light of Peace

Remain Zealous and Seek Me

Bring into your focus
Thoughts of a peaceful life.
Choose to clear your mind
Of all your troubles.
Refresh your soul daily
With My word.
Renew your spirit
By praying fervently.
Remain zealous
And keep seeking to deepen
Your knowledge of Me.
Never stop growing your faith.

Live in My Peace

Beloved child of God,
Lovingly created
In My image,
You were born to shine
And give Me glory.
Continue to live and walk
Each day in peaceful harmony.
Use all of the goodness
I created inside of you,
And you will live
In My peace.

Believe in Your Breakthrough

Believe in your relief
And your breakthrough.
Expect joy and goodness
To come to you.
Choose to see with eyes of faith
And listen with ears of love.
Sometimes it will look like
Life is not going
As you think it should.
Stay calm,
And remain close to Me.
Hold tightly to your faith,
And heed My words.
Trust that you will be okay.
Believe in your breakthrough.

My Response and Commitment

Father, I will always trust You,
Believe in Your word,
Listen to Your warnings,
And follow Your guidance.
Father, I will always honor
Your holy name
And willingly walk
In Your amazing grace.
Father, there are times
When it is hard to find joy
And inspiration,
Especially when I get disheartened.
Father, how will I know what to do?

God's Response:
My Power Lives in You

Blessed child, remain calm.
My love will help keep you strong.
There is never a reason
To be sad or blue,
As I will always love you.
Together, we will walk through your storm.
I will never neglect you or leave you.
Be joyful and remain in good faith.
With Me, you will always be safe.
No matter what you may go through,
Remember, My power lives within you

God will always be with you.

Essay of Thought:
Listen to My Spirit and My Direction

You must listen to My Spirit, watch for My signs, keep reading My word. As long as you do the best that you can do, I will remain supporting and assisting you.

You can improve My connection to you by protecting your space and increasing your time with Me. Your main barrier is that you have not brought your mind to rest, and you are not entirely focused on Me. When you bring your focus back to Me, do not do it in haste. Instead, be purposeful and truly embrace what I mean to your life.

Each day you have opportunities to learn, to grow, and to expand your view of life and happiness. The challenges you face are part of your destiny. You may not always see the beauty in every step of your journey. What you must know is that every one of your steps, trials, hardships, and stumbles were needed to build you into who you are today. Those steps are part of the strength you have gained so far on your journey. Be proud, as I am forever proud of you!

Chapter 5:
The Joy of the Lord is Our Strength

Stay on the right path of truth,
And continue to walk in God's light.

Focus Scripture:

The Lord is my strength and song, and has become my salvation.
— Psalms 118:14 (KJV)

Fill Me Up

Sometimes life gets so hard,
Father, I become tired
And I do not know what to do.
I live by faith, seek understanding,
And survive on Your truth.
Father, I enjoy the cool waters
Of Your love, too.
Please continue filling me up
With Your word.
That way, Father, I know
I will make it through.

God's Guiding Light of Peace

Thank You for My Journey

Lord, thank you
For never leaving my side.
I do not know how
I managed to survive each day,
Pushing away Your grace.
It was never my intention
To disrespect You.
My mind was spinning,
And my world was unsteady.
My vision became unclear,
And I did not rely fully on You.
Thank you for helping me
Live to see all of my new possibilities
In my journey with You.

God's Guiding Light of Peace

God Cares for Us

God loves us,
And He wants us
To live happier lives.
Each day He blesses us
With more of His amazing
And glorious grace.
God strengthens us
When we are weak.
He forgives us
When we are wrong,
And He directs our path
When we are lost.
God is always caring for us.

My Words Bring Comfort

Hold on, My beloved one,
My grace is coming.
Remain faithful, steadfast, true,
And stand firm in what
I have called you to do.
Choose to pay attention
To the best parts of your life.
Let My love flow into you
And allow it to flourish in your heart.
Let My words of comfort
Bring sweet music to your ears
And peace to your soul.

God's Guiding Light of Peace

You Are Covered in My Love

You are My beloved,
And I have covered you
In My love.
Trust that I will provide for you.
I am showing you My grace.
You are looking for something else.
You need only what I provide.
Reflect on your life,
And embrace your joy.
There is always something
To be thankful for.

A Well-Lived Life

Allow faith
To guide every step you take.
Allow joy
To live each day in your heart.
Allow peace
Permanent residence in your mind.
Listen to the hearts of others
To find their true intentions.
Always keep an open mind
And extend a warm hand
Toward your fellow human being
In kindness.
These are the keys to unlocking
The journey of a well-lived life.

God's Guiding Light of Peace

Empowering Affirmations

An Affirmation of Being

My heart is calm.
Clarity is all around me.
I have peace in my mind.
Everything I need
Is already inside of me.
I will achieve my goals.

An Affirmation of Balance

My life is in balance.
I am surrounded
By God's goodness,
And His protection.
Peace lives in my heart.
Joy lives in my soul.

An Affirmation of Worth

I am a child of God.
I was created in His image.
God loves me just as I am.
I am covered in God's grace.
I am surrounded by God's love.

An Affirmation of Peaceful Living

There is joy in my heart.
There is peace in my soul.
There is calm in my mind.
I welcome happiness
Into my life.

An Affirmation of Acceptance

My path is clear,
My future is bright.
I will fulfill my purpose,
And my journey will be great.

An Affirmation of Purpose

I am meeting the world with a smile.
I am totally walking in God's Grace.
Nothing but positivity will come my way.

An Affirmation of Gratitude

I am thankful
For my life.
I appreciate the blessings
Of each new day.
I am prepared
With all I need
To achieve my goals.
I will reach my dreams.

An Affirmation of Happiness

I accept joy and goodness
Into my life.
I appreciate and support
The calm and serenity
Of my mind.
I deserve and embrace
My happiness.

An Affirmation of Joy

I wake up each day
With peace, positivity, and joy
Flowing through me.
Every step I take
Is covered in God's grace.
I live in God's mercy and joy.

An Affirmation of Life

I am thankful
For every blessing I receive.
I release all negativity
And stress from my life.
I welcome and embrace
God's divine energy into my life.

An Affirmation of New Beginnings

I welcome each day of life.
I forgive myself for all previous errors.
I am open to new experiences.
I create my own happiness and joy.
I am responsible for my own peace.

A Place for You to Write an Affirmation
What are you committed to achieve for yourself?
Please list 3-4 thoughts of positive actions or goals.

1.

2.

3.

4.

God is Sending What You Need

God loves and cares
For each of us individually.
He is always watching,
And He is aware
Of our every need.
Never doubt that God
Has unique plans for you.
If you need care,
It is coming to you.
If you need joy,
It is coming to you.
God is sending
Your care, your joy,
And He is sending
Your breakthrough.

Essay of Thought:
Every Day is a Sweet Blessing

Every day of life is a sweet blessing, a gift, and a wonderful opportunity. How well we choose to live our lives is up to us. Each situation is either a choice, a challenge, a lesson, or a combination of all three.

I find that my days are full of learning opportunities. I see life's difficulties as part of a series of progressive life lessons. By looking at my life like a classroom, where God is my teacher, I open myself more to growth and change. Challenges, changes and minor difficulties are usually not a threat, but an important life process. Every day the challenges we encounter give us wonderful opportunities to grow, become stronger, and to learn.

I believe that how much we learn and how much we grow depends on how willing we are to welcome the processes of life. The next time you are faced with difficulties, challenges and/or change, look deeper for the meaning of the situation. Be open and do not resist any positive opportunities for growth.

Since each of us is unique, no one experiences a situation in the exact same way, even when we are standing in the same location. Our life experiences contribute to how we respond to life stressors. A person who grew up in California may not react to a minor earthquake, whereas someone who has never seen or been in a small earthquake may go into a full panic. A person who was bitten by a dog may see every dog as a vicious threat, whereas someone who grew up with dogs sees every dog as a friend.

God's Guiding Light of Peace

Continued

    We must seek to understand the feelings, triggers and emotions behind a person's behavior to be more effective at walking through life and living cohesively in our communities.Sometimes life gets to be a challenge, yet we are still here. We are still walking in victory with God and His Holy Spirit. Be careful not to get distracted or let gloom find you. Hold tightly to your faith, and allow it to continue to guide you.

    You are going to be okay. If you keep joy and faith in your heart, you will find moments of tranquility, peace, and happiness. Keep trusting in your purpose and walking in your truth.

    God is good to us each and every day. From the beautiful sun shining high above, the cooling drops of rain, and the sweet summer breeze, God continues to provide for our every need. I could walk and sing of His sweet praises all day. Smile and continue to trust in God's grace and His promises for your life.

    Each day of your life is filled with wonderful opportunities for joy. Life is meeting you where you are and waiting for you to make the next step. Choose to reach for what you want most, and understand that any battle you may face is already won. Continue to build on your faith daily, and enjoy all of the smiles life will send your way.

God's Guiding Light of Peace

Tips to Live Happier:

1. Choose to be thankful for each day.
2. Greet every day with a smile.
3. Choose to live each day in peace.
4. Commit to always finding the bright side of life.
5. Believe in yourself and in your abilities.
6. Choose to be grateful, and appreciate each blessing.
7. Choose to love, respect and see the beauty in all humanity.
8. Commit to being happy and joyful.
9. Share your joy and kindness with the world.
10. Help everyone whom you have the opportunity to assist.
11. Do what makes your heart sing.
12. Be open and accepting of change.
13. Live in the truth of who you are.

Happiness is meant for you!

Closing Thoughts: Choose to Walk in a Spirit of Gratitude

Sometimes God sends messages in more subtle ways. Today I think He just wanted me to slow down, to understand that not every day will be everything we want it to be. He wanted me to see the beauty of my life as it is and to understand that I may never have everything that I want, though I am never living in a state of lack. God continues to provide daily, and I am grateful for my life.

The choice for us to make is to find joy and give God thanks every day, no matter how much of the day appears not to be going our way. You must trust the journey He laid out for you. Believe in His process and in your purpose.

Not everything is fair, just and nothing in this world is perfect, except for God. You must therefore choose to walk in a spirit of gratitude and always be thankful.

Summary of Thoughts

God speaks to us in many ways: through His word, dreams, visions, silence, and the still small voice. I believe we are all born with a longing inside of our souls to connect with our Higher Power. Which is why many of God's children continue to seek out His comfort and blessings. That is why our souls cry out for Him.

When we choose to pray, we are showing God that we love, care, and appreciate Him. Prayer helps us open up the most profound thoughts of our hearts and our souls to God so He can pour more of His peace and goodness inside of us.

Sometimes in life we can face challenges that can knock us off our feet. With God's strength, love and direction, we can find ways to stand again. We have a choice each day to get back up and to try again.

God has promised that He will not give us more than we can handle. We must believe in ourselves as much as God believes in us.

Your blessings are already apart of you, and I believe that God adds to our blessings each day. So press forward in you life, believe in yourself, grow in love and in knowledge, keep standing, and walk bravely through your journey. God is with you all the way. And we will continue to keep you in our prayers.

— The Poetry from the Heart team

Closing Prayer:
You Are Worthy of Our Praise

Father God,
Please continue to use our lives
As You see fit
To help further Your will.
Please continue to direct our steps,
Keep us safe and protect us
From the many storms
We face every day.
Please continue to align us
With your purpose
So we can be
Of best service to You.
Thank you for bringing me
To a deeper sense of peace
And for allowing me
To live and see
All the fruits of what
You have planted, watered
And grown within me.
Father God,
You are forever and always
Worthy of our praise.
Thank you, God,
For the strength You bring into my life.
We pray this prayer
Through Your Son Jesus Christ's name,
Amen.

Dedication

I dedicate *God's Guiding Light of Peace* to my beautiful family: my amazing grandfather, my loving parents, my awesome siblings, and my wonderful children and grandchildren. Each of you is part of the flame that burns in my heart. You remind me of the goodness that still exists in this world.

Without your love and support, this poetry collection would not be possible. Each word I write is in tribute to you. It is because of your unconditional love and sweet encouragement of me that I continue to grow. You help me to believe in a better way of living, loving, and finding joy. You inspire me to remain strong and encouraged. I will always love, honor, support and encourage you in return.

I must make a special mention of my big brother, Victor Webb, who spoke into my heart that I have a gift, a purpose and an opportunity to write and make a difference in the world. Victor, you have always touched my heart with the kindness of a gentle giant. Thank you for always believing in me and for taking the time to impart wisdom and insight. I love you.

Afterword

We hope you enjoyed the loving thoughts we shared from our hearts. We now ask that you share our words with a friend, and please leave a review on Amazon.com and/or Goodreads.com

About the Author

C. Melita Webb is a lover of life, a mother, and a grandmother who is visually challenged. She has loved words and books all her life. As a student, she excelled in writing deeply touching and reflective prose.

Publishing was a dream she gave up on 30+ years ago, though she continued to write in her heart, mind and spirit. Later, she began speaking and writing into the hearts of her family and friends, too.

In fact, it was at the request of a loved one that the first book was published. She had no idea how powerful her words would still be, or how many had longed to find a voice like hers.

Her writings are full of passion, clarity and purpose. They span many years and phases of life. Each book in her collection tells a story of love, life, and humanity. Included are reflective poems, loving affirmations, supportive prayers, motivational essays, and cries from the heart. She writes the words that live in all our hearts.

God's Guiding Light of Peace is a perfect gift for you, or someone you care for. Please enjoy this collection with our love and best wishes.

— The Poetry from the Heart team

God's Guiding Light of Peace

**Other Poetry from the Heart books
by C. Melita Webb**

Built for God's Glory: Understanding Our Purpose
March 2018
ISBN-13: 978-1986514101
ISBN-10: 1986514102

God Placed You Here: A Walk to Faith
August 2017
ISBN-13: 978-1539816591
ISBN-10: 1539816591

The Light That is You: Conversations of God's Love
October 2016
ISBN-13: 978-1537781358
ISBN-10: 1537781359

All is Redeemed in Truth and Light: Poetry from the Heart
July 2016
ISBN-13: 978-1535329989
ISBN-10: 15353299X

Please visit us at http://www.cmelitawebb.com

Made in the USA
Monee, IL
07 September 2019